The **Essential** Buyer's Guide

MAZDA

MX-5 MIATA

MkI 1989-97 & MkII 1998-2001

Your marque expert:
Carla Crook

T0051550

VELOCE PUBLISHING
THE PUBLISHER OF FINE AUTOMOTIVE BOOKS

Also from Veloce –

www.veloce.co.uk

First published in October 2011 by Veloce Publishing Limited, Veloce House, Parkway Farm Business Park, Middle Farm Way, Poundbury, Dorchester, Dorset, DT1 3AR, England. Fax 01305 250479/ e-mail info@veloce.co.uk/web www.veloce.co.uk or www.velocebooks.com.

ISBN: 978-1-845842-31-4 UPC: 6-36847-04231-8

British Library Cataloguing in Publication Data – A catalogue record for this book is available from the British Library. Typesetting, design and page make-up all by Veloce Publishing Ltd on Apple Mac.
Printed in India by Imprint Digital Ltd.

Introduction
– the purpose of this book

The purpose of this book is to offer a quick, yet detailed and in-depth guide, to finding a Mazda MX-5 matched to your budget, as well as your needs. Always a popular car, there are plenty for sale. Some are honestly described, and owned by enthusiasts, but there are those that are described as being in excellent condition, but hide lots of problems for the next owner. Once you know which model and specification you're after, and how much you're prepared to pay, its time to start reviewing the classified ads, websites, and auction houses to get a feel for the market, and start viewing prospective purchases.

You may have to be prepared to travel a fair distance to find the car that you want, and although it may sound perfect over the telephone, in the flesh it's totally different. Try not to be too disappointed; the right MX-5 is out there for you, and the more you see, the more you can compare and gauge exactly what you are (or aren't) looking for in your ideal MX-5 – your patience and persistence will pay off.

Now in its third generation, the MX-5 first burst onto the automotive scene in 1989, with the original NA 'first generation' model. The MkI, as it's otherwise known, came with a 1.6-litre, four-cylinder, double overhead cam engine at the front, rear-wheel drive, independent double wishbone suspension, front and rear subframes, and light monocoque construction. Recognisable by its pop-up headlights, at the time of its launch, it was the convertible sports car that the world was waiting for. This winning combination has since evolved: the second generation

The original ... a MkI Mazda MX-5.

NB model (referred to as the MkII), was introduced in 1998, and now had fixed headlights, and then, in 2005, the third generation NC cars (MkIII), which, although greatly revised from the original NA cars, still remains true to the ethos of being a small, affordable roadster, with 50/50 front/rear weight balance, and responsive handling. The MX-5 is a modern day classic that's a pleasure to drive, maintain, and own.

This guide covers MkI (NA) cars from 1989-1998, and MkII (NB) cars from 1998-2001. Both the MkI and MkII cars are built on virtually the same platform, with the only differences being cosmetic exterior and interior changes (most notably the headlights), and some revised engine and running gear/chassis features. In essence, they are the same car, sharing the same foibles and advice, but noteworthy differences are highlighted throughout the guide.

For readers outside the UK
Although the model is variously called Miata, MX-5, Eunos, and Roadster around the world, to keep things simple, the model is referred to as the MX-5 throughout this book. However, all models *are* covered.

References to the 'MoT test' refer to an annual official test of roadworthiness that all UK cars are subjected to once they are three years old. Other countries will have similar test regimes and roadworthiness requirements.

Thanks
Without a doubt, I wouldn't have been able to write this book if it weren't for the technical guidance and support of my husband, Tony. Thanks, too, to all my friends at MX5Nutz and the MX-5 Owners' club for their infinite knowledge and assistance, Andy Stott at Autolink, and to the team at Famous Five MX-5s.

Two stunning examples of the MkII Sport edition MX-5, wearing the factory-fitted bodykits.

Essential Buyer's Guide™ currency
At the time of publication a BG unit of currency "●" equals approximately £1.00/ US$1.60/Euro 1.13. Please adjust to suit current exchange rates.

Contents

www.velocebooks.com / www.veloce.co.uk
All current books • New book news • Special offers • Gift vouchers

1 Is it the right car for you?
– marriage guidance

Tall and short drivers
Suitable for all but the exceptionally tall/large driver.

The MX-5 cabin may look small, but those that are tall needn't worry. By fitting a smaller steering wheel, removing the foam from the seats, or swapping to seats from a Lotus Elise, more room can be made.

Weight of controls
Direct, balanced, light steering. Gear change close-ratio and precise, moving easily up and down the gears. The hydraulic clutch is light, as is the brake pedal and accelerator.

Will it fit the garage?
Length: MkI 3975mm/13ft; MkII 3975mm/13ft.
Width: MkI 1675mm/5.49ft; MkII 1680mm/5.51ft.

Interior space
MkI: Front legroom 1085mm/3.55ft; headroom (top closed) 942mm/3.09ft; shoulder room 1280mm/4.19ft.
MkII: Front legroom 1086mm/3.56ft; headroom (top closed) 942mm/3.09ft; shoulder room 1263mm/4.14ft.

Luggage capacity
Boot Capacity: MkI 124 litres; MkII 144 litres.
There's also room on the rear parcel shelf, with the roof up, as well as behind the seats, depending on your driving position.

Running costs
Service intervals at every 6000 miles for MkI, 9000 miles for MkII.

Useability
Ideal as a daily driver, weekend car, or track day toy. Economical fuel consumption, low running costs, Japanese build quality and reliability.

Parts availability
Numeous suppliers the world over, easy availability.

Parts costs
See chapter 2 for further information.

Insurance
The MkI cars can be insured very reasonably on a Classic insurance policy. There are also reductions for members of MX-5 owners clubs.

Investment potential
Although produced en masse, numbers will decline as more and more rusty examples end up in the breaker's yard. Values are currently low, but remain steady; over time, as fewer appear on the road, values will increase. It's most likely that the very limited/special edition models, and early unmodified MkIs, will hold higher values as they become more desirable.

Foibles
Weak crankshaft on the very early MkI cars, and rust issues which can affect the sill/arch areas.

Plus points
Classic British sports car good looks, with Japanese reliability. The soft top can be dropped in a matter of seconds. Very easy to work on and maintain, represents excellent value for money.

Minus points
Low ground clearance, lack of straight line power.

Alternatives
Toyota MR-2, MGF, Fiat Barchetta, Honda CRX Del Sol.

2 Cost considerations
– affordable, or a money pit?

Mechanical parts
Secondhand
Engine x350
Gearbox x100
Alternator x75
Differential x150
Coil pack x50

New
Clutch (parts only) x175
Brake discs (pair, either front or rear) x45
Brake pads (pair, either front or rear) x35
Brake calipers (reconditioned) x110
Electric window regulators x70
Stainless steel manifold x300
Stainless steel exhaust (from Catback) x350
Catalytic converter x150
De-cat pipe x55
Clutch master cylinder x60
Clutch slave cylinder x15
Cylinder head gasket set x75
Battery x75
Coil pack x200-300
HT leads x35
Shock absorber x75
Springs (set 4) x150
Trackrod end x20
Water pump x35

Body parts
Hardtop; secondhand x300, new x1000
Bonnet x200
Front bumper x250
Rear bumper x250
Front wing x125
Rear wing x200
Front headlamp (MkI) x25
Front headlight units (MkII) x220
Rear lights x60
Wheels (set 4) x250
Windscreen/windshield x175
Bootlid x225
Door x300
Seat retrim x250
New hood/roof: vinyl x175, mohair x275

Secondhand parts for the MX-5 are prolific and affordable, with specialist breakers widely spread. Generally, you'll find that secondhand parts are about one quarter of what you'll pay for new parts, so body parts such as bumpers, bonnets, doors, etc are often more economical to buy from a breakers.

The MX-5 is a simple car to work on; it's the perfect car to be run and enjoyed on a budget.

Hardtops are desirable extras. Buying new is very expensive, so most opt to buy secondhand.

Most parts are easy to obtain. Perhaps the most difficult to find (and usually the most sought-after and therefore expensive) are the JDM (Japanese Domestic Market) aftermarket performance and styling accessories.

3 Living with an MX-5
– will you get along together?

If you're looking for a two-seater, open topped sports car, with classic good looks, reliability, affordability, and fantastic handling, then you really need look no further than considering an MX-5. As the world's best selling sports car, The MX-5 is a true testament to itself, with the earlier MkI and MkII models still as affordable as ever. It's a perfect choice not just as a fun and enjoyable daily driver, but as a weekend track car, a project base for a kit car, or for those wishing to exploit the capabilities of the bulletproof engine and super-sweet, responsive handling – it's a tuners dream, with supercharged and turbocharged examples popular.

Dont expect the MX-5 to be a performance sports car. Its brisk in a straight line, but is by no means fast – but that's not what these cars are about. It really comes alive on twisty country lanes, and the engine will rev comfortably up to the 7000rpm red line. MX-5s are nippy around town, and its small size makes parking easy; however, with the roof up, there's a blind spot from the rear quarter view. There's not a huge amount of difference between the 1.6 and 1.8 engines. Having both variants, I find the 1.6 far revier throughout the whole of its range, with the 1.8 having more torque low down in the gears, and just that little bit of extra top end power. MkI 1.8 cars come with larger brakes and extra chassis bracing as standard, and although slightly heavier, there's not much difference in performance.

Mechanically, there's not much that can go wrong with an MX-5. They have a non-interference engine, meaning that if the cam belt snaps, the valves won't crash into the pistons. The MX-5 utilises a similar low compression engine to that used in the Mazda 323 turbo, so lends itself well to forced induction modification. The only weakness with the very early MkI cars, is the potential for crank nose failure (this is detailed further in chapter 7, 15 Minute evaluation).

Suspension is balanced and firm, but shouldn't be harsh, although some aftermarket shocks and lowering springs setups can be hard and stiff. The

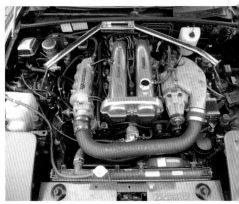

An MX-5 at home on the race track. Many enthusiast-owned cars are regularly taken on trackdays. In the UK there are two official competition racing series: MaX5 Racing and the Ma5da MX-5 Championship.

If you want it all, then there are options out there for supercharging and turbocharging (safely too, as long as the car is properly tuned). This is a 1.8 Jackson Racing Eaton supercharged MkI.

handling can be 'woolly' if the car isn't properly aligned, or has poor, mismatched tyres. Good geometry settings will easily sort any car that's not driving as it should, and the MX-5 benefits from independent double wishbone suspension front and rear, fully adjustable for camber and castor. Owners need to be careful of sharp inclines and over sized speed bumps; the low ground clearance means it's easy to bottom out. Being a traditional rear-wheel drive sports car, the MX-5 is tail end happy if driven hard in the wet, but is by no means uncontrollable. The pinpoint steering provides great feedback, the gearbox is taut, and its close ratio gearchange is renowned for its rifle-bolt precise action. The exhaust note from the standard system is sporty and nicely conspicuous, without being obtrusive.

There are several companies in the UK and USA that specialise in the forced induction field, and can provide all the advice needed in this area. This 1.6 MkI is currently running over 250bhp, and is powered by a Garrett turbocharger.

The interior is simple, yet despite its size, roomy, with deep footwells. The instruments are easy to hand, and the dials are in front of you, where they should be. The gear stick is close by, and the pedals directly in front and nicely spaced (heel-and-toe should be no problem). In the winter, you'll find the heater powerful, taking just a few minutes to make the cabin nice and warm. For a two-seater, there's lots of usable space – boot, behind the seats, and the rear parcel shelf. The MkII has slightly more boot space, with the spare wheel positioned low in the boot floor. As a driver, you sit *in* an MX-5, not on it: it's a low car, so heavy traffic can feel intimidating. The seats are adjustable, and are comfortable and supportive on long drives. With the roof down, the cabin is buffet-free up to around 70mph, with the roof up, it's surprisingly quiet, even at motorway speeds.

The soft top is dropped in seconds, and is raised nearly as quick. If you're strong and tall enough, you may be able to raise it while seated in the cabin. The MX-5 is a popular car, famous for its vibrant community and owners' club scene,

with lots of support and technical expertise to be found online, on various MX-5 forums, and many organised outings, meets, shows and trackdays.

There is no doubt that the highlight of MX-5 ownership is the chance to get out on a long drive. Owners' clubs regularly get together for organised runs, meets, and shows.

4 Relative values
– which model for you?

MkI
UK & Europe
1.6-litre 116bhp engine, 1990 to 1995 **80%**
1.6-litre 88bhp engine, 1995 to 1998 **70%**
1.8-litre 130bhp engine, 1994 to 1995 (Series 1) **90%**
1.8-litre 133bhp engine, 1995 to 1998 (Series 2) **100%**

Eunos Roadster (Japan) and MX-5 Miata (USA, Canada and Australasia)
1.6-litre 116bhp engine, 1989 to 1994 **90%**
1.8-litre 130bhp engine, 1994 to 1995 (Series 1) **90%**
1.8-litre 133bhp engine, 1995 to 1998 (Series 2) **100%**
(MkI 1.8 cars were equipped with larger brakes and additional chassis bracing)

MkII
Worldwide
1.6-litre 110bhp engine, 1998 to 2001 **80%**
1.8-litre 140bhp engine, 1998 to 2001 **100%**

The Eunos Roadster
There are many myths surrounding the Japanese import version of the MX-5. Don't let a dealer fool you into believing Eunos Roadster spares are any different, or more expensive, to a UK model's; they're the same. The Roadsters were undersealed, the same as UK cars; the bonus with the Eunos, is that they were fitted with more extras than their UK cousins, and later imports into the UK are generally rust free. Some insurance brokers charge a higher premium for the Roadster, however, if you choose a specialist MX-5 broker, this shouldn't be an issue.

Visual differences between the 1.6 and 1.8 cars are that the text on the cam cover on the 1.6 engines are inlaid, as shown here ...

... while on the 1.8 cars it's raised.

The best way to tell the difference between a UK car and a Eunos Roadster is to check the VIN number located on the plate on the engine bay firewall. UK and Europe MX-5 chassis numbers start JMZ followed by 14 characters.

Eunos chassis numbers start NA (for MkI), NB (for MkII). In the USA they start JM1 and in Australasia, JMO.

Other visual differences on the MkI are the rear number/licence plate panels, this is a Eunos Roadster ...

... this MkI is a UK model.

The revised interior of a MkII MX-5. Although similar to a MkI, notable differences are the dashboard, and all MkIIs came with airbags as standard.

The original ... a MkI MX-5 with its famous pop-up headlights.

The slate black interior of a Crystal White MkI MX-5.

A MkII MX-5 with its fixed headlights, this is a 10th Anniverary limited edition model of which 7500 were made worldwide, with 600 for the UK market, all with 6-speed gearboxes.

Each country has had various special and limited editions across the whole of the range: these were equipped with extras including different colour paintwork, leather seats, interior trim, and various performance upgrades. This stunning MkI with subtle modifications is a Eunos Roadster VR-Limited Combination A, of which 700 were made in metallic Vin Rouge mica paint.

5 Before you view
– be well informed

To avoid a wasted journey, and the disappointment of finding that the car doesn't match your expectations, be very clear about what questions you want to ask before you pick up the telephone. Some of these points might appear basic, but when you're excited about the prospect of buying your dream classic, it's amazing how some of the most obvious things slip the mind. Also, check classic car magazines for the current values of the model you are interested in, which give both a price guide and auction results.

Where is the car?
Is it going to be worth travelling to the next county, state, or even another country? A locally advertised car, although it may not sound very interesting, can add to your knowledge for very little effort, so make a visit – it might even be in better condition than expected.

Dealer or private sale?
Establish early on if the car is being sold by its owner or by a trader. A private owner should have all the history, so don't be afraid to ask detailed questions.

A dealer may have more limited knowledge of a car's history, but should have some documentation. A dealer may offer a warranty/guarantee (ask for a printed copy) and finance.

Cost of collection and delivery?
A dealer may well be used to quoting for delivery by car transporter. A private owner may agree to meet you halfway, but only agree to this after you have seen the car at the vendor's address to validate the documents. Conversely, you could meet halfway and agree the sale, but insist on meeting at the vendor's address for the handover.

View – when and where?
It's always preferable to view at the vendors home or business premises. In the case of a private sale, the car's documentation should tally with the vendor's name and address. Arrange to view only in daylight and avoid a wet day: most cars look better in poor light or when wet.

Reason for sale?
Do make this one of the first questions. Why is the car being sold, and how long has it been with the current owner? How many previous owners?

Condition (body/chassis/interior/mechanicals)?
Ask for an honest appraisal of the car's condition. Ask specifically about some of the check items described in chapter 7.

All original specification?
An original equipment car is invariably of higher value than a customised version.

Matching data/legal ownership

Do VIN/chassis, engine numbers, and licence plate match the official registration document? Is the owner's name and address recorded in the official registration documents?

For those countries that require an annual test of roadworthiness, does the car have a document showing it complies (an MoT certificate in the UK, which can be verified on 0845 600 5977)?

If a smog/emissions certificate is mandatory, does the car have one?

If required, does the car carry a current road fund license/licence plate tag?

Does the vendor own the car outright? Money might be owed to a finance company or bank: the car could even be stolen. Several organisations will supply the data on ownership, based on the car's licence plate number, for a fee. Such companies can often also tell you whether the car has been 'written-off' by an insurance company. In the UK the following organisations can supply vehicle data:

HPI – 01722 422 422
AA – 0870 600 0836
DVLA – 0870 240 0010
RAC – 0870 533 3660
Other countries will have similar organisations.

Unleaded fuel

If necessary, has the car been modified to run on unleaded fuel?

Insurance

Check with your existing insurer before setting out; your current policy might not cover you to drive the car if you do purchase it.

How you can pay

A cheque/check will take several days to clear, and the seller may prefer to sell to a cash buyer. However, a banker's draft (a cheque issued by a bank) is as good as cash, but safer, so contact your own bank and become familiar with the formalities that are necessary to obtain one.

Buying at auction?

If the intention is to buy at auction see chapter 10 for further advice.

Professional vehicle check (mechanical examination)

There are often marque/model specialists who will undertake professional examination of a vehicle on your behalf. Owners' clubs will be able to put you in touch with such specialists.

Other organisations that will carry out a general professional check in the UK are:
AA – 0800 085 3007 (motoring organisation with vehicle inspectors)
ABS – 0800 358 5855 (specialist vehicle inspection company)
RAC – 0870 533 3660 (motoring organisation with vehicle inspectors)
Again, other countries will have organisations offering similar services.

6 Inspection equipment
– these items will really help

Before you rush out of the door, gather together a few items that will help as you work your way around the car.

This book
This book is designed to be your guide at every step, so take it along and use the check boxes in chapter 9 to help you assess each area of the car you're interested in. Don't be afraid to let the seller see you using it.

Reading glasses (if you need them for close work)
Take your reading glasses if you need them to read documents and make close up inspections.

Magnet (not powerful, a fridge magnet is ideal)
A magnet will help you check if the car is full of filler from previous, cheap repairs. Use the magnet to sample bodywork areas all around the car, but be careful not to damage the paintwork. Expect to find a little filler here and there, but not whole panels.

Torch
A torch with fresh batteries will be useful for peering into the wheelarches and under the car.

Probe (a small screwdriver works very well)
A small screwdriver can be used – with care – as a probe, particularly on the underside. With this you should be able to check any areas of severe corrosion, but be careful – if it's really bad the screwdriver might go right through the metal!

Overalls
Be prepared to get dirty. Take along a pair of overalls, if you have them.

Mirror on a stick
Fixing a mirror at an angle on the end of a stick may seem odd, but you'll probably need it to check the condition of the underside of the car. It will also help you to peer into some of the important crevices. You can also use it, together with the torch, along the underside of the sills and on the floor. You're looking for accident damage, as well as corrosion.

Digital camera
If you have the use of a digital camera, take it along so that later you can study some areas of the car more closely. Take a picture of any part of the car that causes you concern, and seek a friend's opinion.

A friend, preferably a knowledgeable enthusiast
Ideally, have a friend or knowledgeable enthusiast accompany you: a second opinion is always valuable.

7 Fifteen minute evaluation
– walk away or stay?

Exterior

Assess the paintwork carefully, as a respray is often the most costly area to put right. Ensure you're not looking at an MX-5 that has been resprayed from its original colour; anything non-original can devalue it considerably, or be difficult to match should it be a non-standard Mazda colour. Check the rear boot area under the carpets, and the engine bay, as these areas tend to remain in the original colour. Check for any overspray. Look at each of the panels for any ripples, rough paintwork, and to check that the colour on each panel matches.

Sills/rockers are the one weakness of the MX-5 – this is where rust can really take hold. For the rear sill, look at the area around the two drain holes for any bubbling or established rust; this is where corrosion usually starts, as the drain holes can block up over time, and prevent water escaping. The rust will start from within and work its way out, so what may appear to be just paint bubbling is the rust working its way from inside. Also, you will need to bear in mind that if there is substantial rust, not only will the outer sills need to be repaired, but the inner sills may need replacing too. The only solution to rusty sills, is for all the corrosion to be cut away, and new steel welded in place. Costs vary depending on how much work needs to be done, and usually starts from about ⬤x150 per sill. Ensure the drain holes are clear (use a paperclip to insert into the holes); there are eight in total, two on the front of the sills, two on the rear. If blocked (or, worse, if you can hear water sloshing in the sill area on a test drive), and rust hasn't appeared as yet, rust is almost certainly imminent. Corrosion starts around the drain holes, and, on the front sills, spreads towards

Lacquer peel on the rear bumper of a MkII. A defect such as this should be easily rectified by a body shop, or a replacement black bumper could be sought. However, if this is affecting any other panels then you will need to factor in the possibility of a full respray.

Here you can see the drain holes on the rear sill of a MkI – there are eight in total on the MX-5. This is also the key jacking point of the car (jack supplied in the boot). Look for rust around this area. The drain holes will block over time.

the lower half of the front wing. Look all the way along the sills, and check along the underneath seam line for any bubbling or holes. Be wary of MX-5s with side skirts; when fitted, these cover the sills and will hide any rust.

On both MkI and MkII models, the front wings bolt on, and are easily replaced. Look for rust around the arch area, on the front of the wing above the bumper, and also where the wings attach to the sills.

Take a look at the rear wings; the most important area to check here, is around the wheelarch, for rust and bubbling. Check for dents; rear arches can be difficult areas to repair, as, although replacement rear arches are available, they are not bolt-on, and need to be welded into place.

Look around the A-pillar/windscreen surround and scuttle for rust. Check the hood, which will be either vinyl or mohair. If vinyl, check for cracks, rips or splits. These can appear anywhere on the roof, from the rear plastic window, to the edges where it folds when in the down position. If there are cracks or splits, it's likely that these will leak, or, at the least, allow damp and moisture into the cabin.

Soft top roof drain holes reside in the corners, near the seatbelt turrets. When feeling whether they are clear, you may need to have the roof half up, as they are tricky to get to. Clear them by using curtain wire or similar, to allow water to drain via the rear wheelarch.

Interior
Check inside to make sure any wear on the seats is consistent with the car's current mileage. Have a look at the carpets for wear, and also feel behind the seats and in the footwells for signs of damp. If there is wetness or watermarks, then either the roof could be leaking, the soft top drain holes may be blocked, or the rain rail is poorly fitted, preventing water properly draining away, causing it to run into the cabin. If you can, look beneath the carpets, as they are waterproof, and any

Check the seats, which will be either cloth or leather, for wear on the bolsters.

ingress of water may still be evident beneath, even if the top appears dry. Check the top of the dash for cracks and splits; sun damage can effect this area.

Boot/trunk
The MX-5 boot area is carpeted, and is fitted with a spare wheel. The battery is fixed to the right, with a carpet cover which poppers over. A jack and handle resides in its own compartment to the left, under the boot carpet, along with a basic toolkit and wheel brace. The MkII's boot layout is slightly different, with a little extra space. Check under carpets for any rust, and particularly check around the battery area, for signs of spillage and subsequent corrosion. Feel for dampness to the carpets; the seals/gaskets to the rear lights can deteriorate, as can the seal to the car aerial, and allow rainwater to enter.

Check along the channels around the boot for rust, and look at the boot lid itself, for any dents where careless owners may have overloaded the boot with shopping and slammed the lid shut.

The battery should be clamped in place to prevent movement. Some cars may have not had the battery secured properly, so check the rear wing for damage (dents, paint rippling, or cracking). MX-5s should be fitted with gel batteries, to prevent risk of spillage and corrosion.

Mechanicals

An MX-5's engine is as durable and reliable as you will find, but as with any engine, it must be regularly maintained and looked after. Engines will happily run past the 200,000 mark and onwards – a true testament to its bulletproof nature. However, it's still very important to make some key checks to the health of the engine. Look at all of the fluid levels and condition. Oil should be a nice golden colour; if it's very black, the car will be seriously overdue for an oil change. Check the radiator (fluid should be at the top), expansion tank (should be half full – if empty, there could be a coolant leak), brake fluid, and power steering reservoir. Check the oil dipstick for visible contaminants; be wary of anything resembling metallic particles (best walk away if this is the case). Look for water in the oil, or vice versa. Check for emulsified oil under the oil filler cap (it looks like mayonnaise), as this could be a sign of water getting into the oil, indicating possible head gasket failure. (Bear in mind, though, that this can appear on cars which have only ever been used for short journeys.) If any, or all of the fluids are clearly dirty, it's usually a sign the car hasn't been well cared for.

Factor in that you will need to get all these fluids changed should you buy the car. Generally, poor maintenance is indicative of potential problems for the future, something you will need to consider if you do decide to buy. Take a look at all of the fan belts, and check for cracks and wear. Check for excessive wear on the water pump pulley; rock it back and forth – if there's movement, a change may soon be due. Water pump and cam belt are often changed at the same time, as a similar strip-down is required when fitting either, so labour costs are saved by carrying out both together.

Early MX-5s (1989-Aug 1990) have a potential weakness with their crankshafts. The crankshaft pulley woodruff key can wear, causing eventual crankshaft failure. The best way to identify if the car you are viewing has the potentially faulty crank, is to check to see how many slots the pulley has. If it has four slots, it's the earlier, weaker, short-nose pulley; if it has eight slots, it's the later, improved, long-nose design. If you're considering a car with the four-slot pulley, you can check for wear by looking for wobble from the crankshaft pulley whilst the engine is running. If there is wobble, and the car is experiencing low speed loss of power or hesitation, this could also be a symptom of crankshaft wear. The only fixes are either a replacement engine, or, enthusiasts have been known to cure worn woodruff keyways with Loctite – commonly known as the 'Loctite fix.'

Take a look around the engine, checking for any visible oil leaks. The cam sensor O-ring, which is located at the rear of the engine, can leak and weep oil. However, if this does need replacing, it's a nice, easy job. Check MkI 1.8 cars, as any leakage from the O-ring can drip onto the rear heater hose, making it porous and causing coolant loss. Top end oil leaks, from around the cam cover, can also occur; a new gasket should resolve this.

Check all the hoses; look for perishing, chafing, holes, or splits.

Lastly, whilst you are here, check the chassis numbers on the VIN plate, on the firewall/bulkhead, to ensure you're looking at the correct model MX-5.

Underneath

Okay, you may get dirty here! Check the general structure beneath the car.

Look up underneath the front bumper; be aware of any bent metal. Look for engine or gearbox oil leaks, and structural rust or heavy corrosion (I once viewed an MX-5 which was so rusty underneath, it looked like it had been underwater all its life!) Now, check the chassis rails and floorpan; you'll want to look at these areas carefully (this is where your torch will come in handy), checking for rust and holes. If you have the previous MoT certificates, were there any advisories relating to corrosion in the key areas, such as seatbelt mountings (which reside in the rear arches)? If so, look at these areas carefully. Can you see any previous repairs or welding? Check to what standard the work

If you can see springs, anti-roll bars, drop links, and wishbones as clean as these on this MkI, then you are looking at an excellent example of a rust-free chassis.

has been completed. Look closely at the chassis rails (so-called chassis rails – they're not structural parts of the car). If the car you are viewing has been lowered, you may notice dents where the car has bottomed out, as well as damage caused by careless mechanics jacking up the car. Check the shock absorbers for signs of leakage or misting. Often, the rubber-ribbed shock boots will be perished; this isn't anything to be concerned about, and their only requirement is to keep the shocks dust and dirt free. Check the springs all around; make sure none are cracked or broken. Look at the front and rear wishbones, and also the front and rear antiroll bars. Ensure none are bent or out of place, and although some surface corrosion may be present, you don't really want to see components which are heavily rusted.

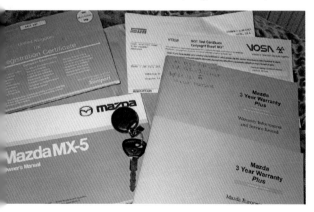

Make sure all paperwork is in place and that VINs match. If the car has an immobiliser be sure to ask whether there are any spare transponders. If it's a Thatcham approved system and there is a certificate, this will make savings on your insurance. It's often a requirement on a convertible car.

Paperwork

Check with the owner that the V5C is present (the USA equivalent is called a 'pink slip'), and ensure the document is in the current owner's name. Check that the VIN numbers match with those on the plate on the engine firewall. It's also worth checking the V5C to see how many previous owners the car has had, and if it's an import, when it was brought into the UK. Eunos Roadsters can be registered with the DVLA as MX-5s, but bear in mind that even if the V5C says it's an MX-5, the VIN plates will clearly show it's a Eunos Roadster. Make sure you insure it as an import, otherwise, should an accident happen, and you have declared the wrong model, you could invalidate your policy and any claim.

Take the car for a drive

This is where you should look for any potential issues.

Start up the engine. The MX-5 has hydraulic lash adjustors (tappets, or HLAs); they can rattle for a few seconds whilst the oil is coming through, but they should soon stop. If you can still hear them after a few minutes, then take the car for a run: if the engine is still rattling on its return, the car is seriously due an oil change, and one can assume it has not had regular oil changes and flushes. Check the exhaust for smoke. Blue smoke may indicate worn valve stem seals or piston rings. White smoke may indicate that there is water entering the cylinders, and is often a sign that the head gasket is leaking.

If an MX-5 drives and handles particularly poorly, and there isn't anything structurally untoward, it's most likely that the car's suspension geometry and/or wheel alignment is out. Once correctly set up for the road or track, the difference can be quite phenomenal.

Once the engine has warmed up, rev the engine slowly. Listen for any knocking sounds that appear at certain rpm levels, and then fade off. Take the car for a test drive with the roof up; you'll hear any untoward noises more clearly. Be aware of any loss of power, hesitation, or misfire. Feel the clutch and test through all the gears several times. Try the brakes; ensure they have a solid feel, and that the car stops in a straight line. Be aware of how the car feels going into corners and how the car travels at speed. Make mental notes of anything untoward which should arise during the test drive, and be sure to use these points as part of your bargaining to get the car at the right price for your budget, should this be the car for you.

www.velocebooks.com / www.veloce.co.uk
All current books • New book news • Special offers • Gift vouchers

8 Key points
– where to look for problems

Look under the carpet in the boot, and check that there's no rust or corrosion from battery spills.

A hood/soft top in this condition will need replacing sooner rather than later, as the damp and resulting mould will affect the interior.

If you can see bubbling to the sills, then the rust is working its way from the inside.

Holes in the underside of the floorpan and inner sill, to this extent, can be costly to repair.

These rear arches are showing the first signs of rust.

This is a four-slot crankshaft pulley, seen on 1989-1991 MkI MX-5s, and is of a weaker design. Check which is fitted to the vehicle you're viewing, regardless of year, as a later 1.6 car may have had a replacement engine fitted from an earlier model.

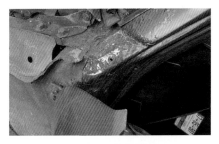

As a comparison, this is the eight-slot revised crankshaft pulley, fitted to MkI cars from mid-1991 onwards.

The A-pillars have been known to rust. Check around the windscreen and down into the scuttle panels for evidence of bubbling.

Side skirts are a popular modification, but can hide any rust present on the sills.

Score each section according to the values in the boxes: 4 = excellent; 3 = good; 2 = average; 1 = poor.
The totting up procedure is detailed at the end of the chapter. Be realistic in your marking!

Paintwork ☐4 ☐3 ☐2 ☐1

It's important to assess the paintwork closely on any prospective car, as a respray is often the most costly area to put right on an MX-5. First, ensure that you're not looking at an MX-5 which has been resprayed from its original colour; anything non-original can devalue it considerably, or at the least, be difficult to match should it be a non-standard Mazda colour.

The engine bay, and the area beneath the boot carpets, tend to remain the original colour after a respray, so check for overspray here. To check if the car is the correct colour, you can obtain the paint code from the engine VIN plate. This is on the rear firewall in the engine bay (for Eunos), or from the sticker sometimes found on the driver's side doorshut (for UK and Eunos). Across the MX-5 colour range, red cars tend to fade and dull more than any other colour. Another common paint defect is for the lacquer to peel or craze, or the paint to flake away, so be sure to check every panel carefully.

A VIN sticker plate as found in the driver's door. Note the paint code 'SU' which indicates Classic Red.

Body panels ☐4 ☐3 ☐2 ☐1

All gaps should be even, the seams smooth, and matched well. Check the panels for ripples, rough paintwork, or patches welded onto the sill. Check that all the panel's colours match; are there any areas that look more freshly painted than others?

Bumpers ☐4 ☐3 ☐2 ☐1

Standard bumpers are polypropylene; check they are securely fitted. Aftermarket front bumpers are popular, and are often made of fibreglass; look for cracks or splits, and check for a good fit, as some can be bodged into place. There may also be a lip spoiler fitted – a desirable extra. Check the bumper reflectors/side markers are present and

Aftermarket Japanese market front bumper, this one is made from fibreglass. This car also comes with optional front fog lights.

screwed in. In the USA, the side markers must be lit to comply with regulations, so check that they work when the side lights/main beam are on.

Check the rear bumper for a good fit; sometimes, the inner ballast section can be missing, resulting in a poorly attached bumper. Are the bumper reflectors/side markers in place, and screwed in tightly? On US cars, ensure they work when main beam/sidelights are on.

Standard front bumper with optional front lip spoiler.

MkI bonnet/hood hinges. These are in good condition, but some can rust and seize. Regular lubrication will keep them operating perfectly.

Bonnet/hood [4] [3] [2] [1]

MX-5 bonnets are made from aluminium. Check bonnet alignment: sometimes, the rear bonnet hinges seize, causing the bonnet to move out of place

Wings/fenders [4] [3] [2] [1]

On both models, the front wings are bolted on, and are easily replaced. Look for rust around the arch area, on the front of the wing above the bumper, and also where the wing attaches to the sill/rocker area of the car. An arch liner should be in place; check where the wing fixes to the engine bay area to make sure all the bolts are present

Rust on a MkI front wing/ fender. Replacement with a new or secondhand wing is more cost-effective than repair.

For the rear, the most important area to check is around the wheelarch and lip, for rust and bubbling. Feel along the arch edge; is there a build up of dirt and mud? Check for dents, as the rear arches can be difficult areas to repair (unlike the front wings, the rears require welding).

A-pillar & windscreen surround [4] [3] [2] [1]

On early UK cars, the A-pillars, windscreen surround, and scuttle should be checked for signs of rust; look for any bubbling.

Wipers [4] [3] [2] [1]

Ensure they work on all settings, and that the screen washers work. Blades may need replacing if the screen is not clearing sufficiently.

Windscreen [4] [3] [2] [1]

Check all window rubbers and seals for perishing. Make sure that the windscreen doesn't have cracks or chips which may need repairing.

Doors [4] [3] [2] [1]

Often the area that sustains the most car park dents. Check all around for any dents or damage. Check along the bottom of the door for rust, and also look into the door

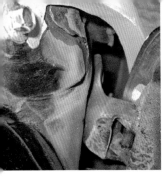

Check the door shuts for rust on the inner wing.

shut area, where the door connects to the car. Check around the inner wing, particularly the area where the inner wing is bolted to the car, for rust or bubbling. In wet weather, this is where the water will run off, and can be a little-known rust hotspot.

Check the condition of the glass. If electric mirrors, check they are working; the switch is on the right-hand side of the dash.

If fitted, check that electric windows work properly, as the motors can burn out, or the cables can snap, rendering the window inoperable. Manual window winders can also seize up, requiring replacement cables.

Locks & keys

Ensure that the doors open and lock correctly. Some cars have a spring connecting the lock to the handle, that can break or come away, preventing the key from opening the lock. Locks can become stiff over time; a little WD-40 can remedy this.

Most MX-5s were supplied with two keys from new; the main master key, which operates all of the locks, and a secondary 'valet' key, which only operates the ignition and driver/passenger doors. Ideally, you'll want a full set; one master key, and a spare/valet key. Check that the keys operate all of the locks correctly.

If you have only the valet key, a new main key can be cut using the code from the door lock barrel, inside the driver's door.

Kickplates   ④ ③ ② ①

MX-5s have either chrome or black plastic kickplates covering the tops of the sills/rockers. Check the edges and corners of the plates where they meet the paintwork, as surface rust can develop where water runs underneath.

Eunos Roadsters and some special edition UK spec MX-5s have chrome door kickplates. Surface rust can appear along the edges, but is not difficult to treat.

Front sills   ④ ③ ② ①

Check the area around the two drain holes for bubbling or established rust. Remember; if you see rust breaking though, it will need attention sooner rather than later, to prevent the corrosion spreading.

This MkI has rust coming through the front sills/rockers and the lower front wing/fender. The sill has also started to collapse where corrosion has caused a weakness at the drain holes/ jacking point.

Rear sill corrosion on the same MkI as shown on the previous page. All of the drain holes were blocked, and, as a result, the rust was evident on each corner.

A MkII with rust just starting to appear on the rear of the sill.

Rear sills ④ ③ ② ①

The rear sills corrode in the same way as the front sills, with rust generally starting around the drain holes, and then spreading out towards the rear wing. Look all the way along the sills, as the rust can spread forward, too. Check along the underneath seam line for any bubbling, or holes where the rust has taken hold.

Rust on the lower rear arch and into the sill of a MkII.

Boot/trunk external area ④ ③ ② ①
Check rain channels for rust, any filled holes on the boot lid deck area, where spoilers may have previously been fitted, or for surface rust on the top or underside of bootlid itself. If the model has a rear brakelight built into the bootlid, ensure this is working. As the boot area is quite shallow, it's not difficult to overfill the boot, and then try to force the bootlid shut, so check for dents or damage.

Boot/trunk internal area ④ ③ ② ①
Spare wheel
Ensure the spare wheel is screwed in place and in good condition, should you ever need to use it!

MkI jack and tool kit in the rear boot recess ...

Toolkit
All MX-5s came with an eight-piece toolkit in a vinyl wrap; check if one is included. There should also be a jack, screwed into place in the well under the carpet on MkI cars, and a handle, attached to the left-hand front boot wall.

... check if the car you are viewing still has its original jack, toolkit and spare wheel.

Boot carpets
Check beneath the carpets for rust, and particularly check around the battery area, for signs of spillage and subsequent corrosion. Feel for dampness to the carpets, as the seals/gaskets to the rear lights, and the aerial, can deteriorate, allowing

rainwater to leak in. Whilst in the boot, check if the car has an electric aerial, that it's operational, and that it raises/lowers correctly.

A MkII's battery is recessed into the boot floor. Acid spillage or ingress of water can cause rust in this area.

Battery ☐ ☐ ☐ ☐

The battery should be clamped in place to prevent movement. Check the rear wing for damage (dents/paint rippling or cracking) which could have occurred due to a loose battery. Sometimes, larger batteries can be fitted, but not properly secured due to their size. The battery should ideally be of the gel type – if it's not, and a wet battery is in situ, check that the battery vent tubes are all in place, otherwise there is a real risk of spillage and corrosion.

Most important is to ensure that the battery is secured, as is the case here.

Fuel filler lid ☐ ☐ ☐ ☐

The fuel filler lid is operated by a release catch in the centre console. Ensure this works, and that the screw-in fuel cap is present.

Lighting ☐ ☐ ☐ ☐
Headlights

With the MkI cars, when the headlights are lowered, do the headlight lids sit flush? Careless mechanics can lean on them, causing the headlight lid to be 'out' along the back edge with the bonnet. However, they are easily pulled back into place. Check that the headlights raise and lower correctly. There are two switches that do this: one is on the right-hand stalk on the steering column, and opens the lids when the lights are switched into the 'main beam' position. The other is beneath the hazard button on the dashboard, and raises the lids but doesn't turn on the bulbs. Should

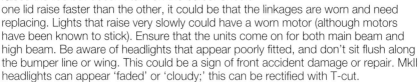

Should the pop-up headlights not work on a MkI, then there are manual winders in the engine bay to lower and raise them.

one lid raise faster than the other, it could be that the linkages are worn and need replacing. Lights that raise very slowly could have a worn motor (although motors have been known to stick). Ensure that the units come on for both main beam and high beam. Be aware of headlights that appear poorly fitted, and don't sit flush along the bumper line or wing. This could be a sign of front accident damage or repair. MkII headlights can appear 'faded' or 'cloudy;' this can be rectified with T-cut.

Side lights, indicators
Ensure all lights are working, and that the units are securely screwed in place.

Rear lights
Check these are working correctly – brake, reverse, and indicators.

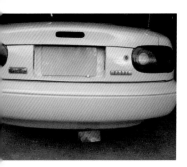

Part of your checklist when looking at a Eunos Roadster is to make sure fog lights are operational. Fog lights are not a requirement in Japan, and most are retro fitted onto imports on arrival in the UK.

Front fog lights
Some cars are fitted with front foglights; they may – or may not – be wired up. If they are, check that they are working; the switch should reside on the dashboard, to the right of the steering wheel.

Rear fog light
Check this works. If the car is an import, make sure that a fog light has been fitted (it's not a legal requirement on Japanese cars). Ensure that there is a corresponding switch in the cabin to operate the fog light.

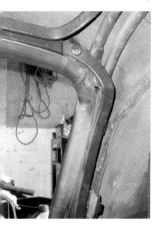

Check the inside of a roof, not just the outside. The interior seams can come loose, glue can become unstuck, and mould/ fungus from a wet cabin can deteriorate the fabric.

Soft top & frame [4] [3] [2] [1]
MkI and MkII cars came with vinyl roofs as standard, sometimes with an upgraded rear glass heated screen, instead of the usual plastic. Mohair hoods are a popular aftermarket choice. Check the roof all over, not just outside but inside, too. Look for splits, holes, and brittle patches, particularly in the key areas along the edge of the roof. On mohair hoods, look for bald patches in the areas where the hood folds. Ensure the fit is snug, that the roof raises and lowers without difficulty, and that the latches are not stiff to close and open. With the roof up, check the drainholes for potential blockages. Ask the seller if the car comes with the optional tonneau cover (most do).

A mohair hood with glass rear window on a MkI.

A very cloudy rear plastic window on a MkI car. This vinyl roof is starting to split on the edges.

Rear window [4] [3] [2] [1]
Care should be taken with the rear plastic window, as, over time, it can become brittle and liable to cracking in cold weather. Ensure that the zip on the rear window is working. Check around the seams for loose stitching, and check the rear window for clouding or cracks.

Hardtops fit to an MX-5 with catches at the front, as well as catches and striker plates on the sides next to the seatbelt turrets. The soft top just folds down to the rear, and does not need to be removed for the hardtop to be fitted.

Hardtop 4 3 2 1

Hardtops are desirable items, particularly in the winter when secondhand prices for them soar. They're excellent for security, keep the car warm, and slightly less noisy, and offer better visibility compared with the soft top. They also stiffen the cabin. The rear glass screens are available heated or non-heated. If the car comes with its hardtop, check that the front and side latches are present, as well as the rear chrome plates. The chrome plates should come with little screws: when taken out, you can move the plate top across, exposing bolts that adjust the hardtop, once in place on the car.

The car should also have side latches on the interior trim, near the seatbelt towers and the rear Frankenstein bolts for the chrome plates to attach to. If the hardtop has a heated rear screen, there's a plug-and-play wiring loom, that connects with a plug on the rear parcel shelf. Not all cars are equipped with the plug – nor, indeed, the heated window switch on the dash – so check this if you're intending to use the heated rear screen.

For extra safety and security, the rear of a hardtop fixes to the outside of the car on 'frankenstein' bolts, which screw into the deck plates.

The interior cabin, dash, and instruments of a MkI Gleneagles limited edition, styled with interior chrome upgrades and additional instrument gauges to the A-pillar.

Seats 4 3 2 1

Depending on the model, MX-5s will have either cloth or leather seats. Most of the Eunos Roadster models have headrest speakers; check that these are working and wired-up (the connecting plug is under the seat). Check for the usual wear and tear (the driver's bolster is usually a good indicator). If you're looking at what appears to be a low mileage car, and the driver's seat is particularly worn, then it could have had its mileage altered. Check that all the runners are operational, and that both seats move freely forwards and backwards.

Carpets 4 3 2 1

Look for rips, general wear and tear, and for signs of dampness behind the driver's seat or in the footwells. A damp footwell could, potentially, cause ECU problems, as the ECU resides behind a plate in the passenger footwell. The carpets are waterproof, so, if you can, check underneath: the carpet may appear dry on top, but could be wet below. Most MX-5s and

Roadsters came with fitted floormats, and it's good to have these to protect the footwell carpets.

Door cards

These pop on and off the door with plastic fixings. The vinyl can become scuffed or torn over time, so check condition. Some limited edition MkI models came with brushed alloy/stainless teardrop speaker surrounds. Speakers sit in the doors, beneath the door cards, so check that they are fitted and are working.

Door cards on a MkI limited edition S-Special Roadster.

Interior lights

Early MkI interior lights are in the footwells; later MkI and MkII interior lights are situated above the rear-view mirror. Check these are present and working.

Rear-view mirror

Early MkI rear-view mirrors are fixed on the inside windscreen surround; later MkI and MkII rear-view mirrors are fixed to the window. Check they are securely in place, and that the glass isn't cracked.

Dash & radio/Stereo

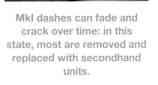

On MkI cars, the top of the dash can sometimes crack due to sun damage, and the black coating can peel, flake, or become scratched off.

Ensure you have the security code, and check that the unit is working. If the car is an import, and still has the original stereo system, it may be difficult to obtain a full range of radio stations (an expander will be required to fix this).

MkI dashes can fade and crack over time: in this state, most are removed and replaced with secondhand units.

Steering wheel & horn

The type of steering wheel depends on the model. Early MkIs came with a Momo steering wheel (the centre cover comes away, revealing the Momo logo, and horn); late MkIs had a standard black steering wheel, with airbag; and some limited editions came with a wooden or a black Nardi steering wheel. You'll often find the original steering has been replaced with an aftermarket version. Check that the car horn is working.

This is a Nardi leather steering wheel as found on some of the Eunos limited edition cars.

Some MkIs came with optional factory-fitted aluminium pedal covers. This car is also fitted with Japanese Domestic Market floor mats, which were optional on the Eunos Roadsters, and came in several different designs.

Pedals 4 3 2 1

Check that there's the right amount of wear for the mileage. If you can, look for fatigue cracks in the pedal box: this allows the accelerator to flex, preventing full throttle. Some limited editions came with aluminium pedal and footrest covers.

Wheels 4 3 2 1

The basic, standard wheels on the MkI and MkII MX-5s are 14in, however, some limited edition MkI cars also came with 15in wheels (an optional factory upgrade for both models). There have been many discussions about the optimum wheel size for an MX-5, and the general consensus is that 15in alloys are best for driveability and handling. Alloy wheels are one of the most popular modifications, so many come with aftermarket sets, and the limited/special editions often came with alloys specific to their model. Check each of the wheels: look under the centre caps, if there are any (these often go missing), ensure all four wheel nuts are in place, and look closely for any severe damage or kerbing to the rims.

Tyres 4 3 2 1

Assess the tyres, ensuring that they're all legal. Do all four tyres match, or are they mismatched, and an unknown make? Tyres can make or break the handling, and well made tyres are key. Tyre pressures should be set at 26psi all round.

These are the standard fitment 14in alloys as found on most MkIs, otherwise known as 'daisies.'

Beautiful BBS 15in alloys wheels, which came as standard on several of the Eunos Roadster limited editions.

Usual brake checks are the pads and discs, but check the brake hoses, too, as the original fitments may be corroded.

Brake discs & pads ④ ③ ② ①
Check the brake discs for wear and scoring, and the pads to see how much wear is left. Replacement pads and discs are economical. 1.8 cars will have larger discs and pads than the 1.6 models. Some cars, if stood for a while, may have seized callipers, although new or reconditioned ones can be easily purchased. Check that the handbrake is working.

Cam belt ④ ③ ② ①
The cam belt should be changed every 60,000 miles, or every five years. Check with the owner when this was last done; if they don't know, it may be worth factoring this into any negotiation. However, it's important to note that the MX-5 engine is 'non-interference,' so should the belt break, the pistons and valves won't collide with each other (although the car will still cease to run, and a tow will be necessary).

Engine bay of a MkII, virtually the same layout as the MkI.

Alternator/power steering belt ④ ③ ② ①
Check both belts for perishing or cracks that would indicate a change is due soon.

Fuel lines ④ ③ ② ①
Check that the rubber hoses aren't perished, split, or have leaks.

MkI engine bay with strut brace and aftermarket induction chamber and air filter.

Radiators should have clean-looking coolant (green, pink or blue in colour), never rusty or dirty ... and never overfilled, as this radiator has been.

Radiator, hoses & fan

From cold, check the radiator fluid level to ensure it's topped-up sufficiently. If it looks brown and rusty, it may not have been changed for a long time. Make sure all the hoses you can see aren't perished, and are firmly fitted with hose clips/jubilee clips. With the car running, check for leaks from the radiator and hoses.

Washer bottle

Check it's in place, and, if empty, top it up and check it's working. The washer bottles on MkI cars with ABS were mounted behind the front bumper, where the brackets can corrode, causing the bottle to drop onto the road: be sure to check the condition.

Exhaust manifold

Standard manifolds generally have a heat shield covering. On aftermarket manifolds, you'll clearly be able to see the stainless steel manifold tubes. Check the manifold is fitted correctly, as the heat shields can work loose, rattle, and leak.

Crankshaft pulley

An important check! Look to see if the pulley is a weaker four-slot, short-nose design, or the stronger, eight-slot, long-nose. If a four-slot, start the car and look for wobble of the crankshaft pulley whilst the engine is running.

Standard exhaust manifolds are hidden away under this heat shield, which can sometimes work loose and cause engine bay rattles.

Water pump

Check for leaks at tickover; they'll run down and come out underneath where the crank pulley is situated. Movement in the water pump is another sign that it may need replacing.

Fluids

Power steering fluid
Ensure the fluid level is correct.

Check the oil for evidence of water ingress. This example is fine.

The main fuse box is in the engine bay, and has a cover that identifies each of the fuses in place.

The main black 80-amp fuse screws in place from underneath the fuse box; all other fuses are push in/ pull out.

Brake fluid

Ensure the correct level in the reservoir. Brake fluid should be between maximum and minimum levels. Check the colour, too: it should be light and golden.

Clutch fluid

If the level is low, this usually means a leaking slave cylinder.

Coolant expansion tank

Ensure there's no oil contamination, and, ideally, that the tank is half full: if it's empty, the car may have a coolant issue. If the water is particularly brown with rust staining, it's likely the car has not been subject to regular antifreeze additive changes.

Oil level & condition

Evidence of oil leaks

Look closely for oil leaks. Obvious places are the rear of the engine (cam seal), and around the cam cover (perished gasket).

Dipstick

Look at the condition of the oil, feeling the fluid between your fingers for any evidence of tiny metal particles.

Filler cap

Check underneath the cap for emulsified oil (evidence of water in the oil). Bear in mind that some is to be expected on a car that has done lots of short trips.

Engine fuse box

Check that all the all fuses are in place; the top of the fuse box lid details the fuses that should be present.

General structure underneath the car ④ ③ ② ①

Look up underneath the front bumper. Be aware of any bent metal caused by accident damage. Check that the car's plastic undertray is in place (often missing), as this protects the engine, and also assists with airflow to optimise cooling. Look for engine oil leaks, gearbox oil leaks, and water leaks (the core plug can leak). Look down the length of the underside, for rust or heavy corrosion.

MkII cars suffer rust on the front chassis legs, as seen here ...

... and here, the same car viewed from the other side.

Chassis and suspension

Chassis rails

Look closely at the chassis rails. These often take a hammering, as the cars sit low and easily bottom out, so ensure any damage has not resulted in severe rust or holing. Sometimes, careless mechanics use this area to jack up the car, and, subsequently, the rails can cave in.

Chassis legs

On MkII cars particularly, check for rust in the front chassis legs, which are situated around the anti-roll bar mounts. They're double thickness steel which, unfortunately, seems susceptible to rot. It can be rectified, but it's a difficult area to fix.

Chassis rails can suffer abuse from bottoming out, but also from rust and corrosion.

Floorpan

Check this area carefully, looking for rust and holes. Can you see signs of previous repairs or welding? If so, check to what standard the work has been carried out. Damage in this area will certainly affect the rigidity and handling, and, as this is a structural area, will cause an MoT fail.

When underneath the car, check the suspension components carefully – rust, corrosion, and worn-out bushes may be evident, as seen here.

Differential & driveshafts

Look for differential oil leaks, and check the rubbers on the universal joints, at the ends of the driveshafts, for any that are perished: they will cause MoT failure.

Brake hoses & pipes

Look closely for oil leaks from the brake hoses. Obvious places are the rear of the engine (cam seal), and around the cam cover (perished gasket).

Hoses can perish and split, causing an MoT failure. Most cars benefit from an upgrade to braided stainless steel hoses.

Brake pipes can corrode, so check carefully. Copper upgrades are a popular replacement.

Steering rack

Check for leaks on the power steering unit. For both manual and power racks, feel/look for any play, move the steering wheel, and compare the movement to that of the front wheels.

Shock absorbers

Check for evidence of leakage. Check that each of the shocks have bump stops. It may be the case that the car you're viewing has aftermarket shocks. Standard shocks are black, or can be yellow Bilstein units, as fitted on the special/limited edition models; aftermarket ones come in a variety of different colours, and may have a dial to adjust the damping. Aftermarket shocks may be height adjustable, too. Generally, you'll be able to tell if a car is lowered if the top of the tyre is about

A MkI car with aftermarket shocks and springs.

a half inch away from the arch lip (also a good indication that the car is fitted with aftermarket suspension). Look at the suspension bushes; on old units they're likely to be perished and worn.

Springs

Ensure there are no cracked or broken springs. Original components may appear very corroded, and, as a result, can be weak. Consider that replacements may be necessary, should this be the case.

CV joint boots

Worn or perished components will fail a UK MoT, so check condition carefully.

Wishbones

Look at the upper and lower wishbones. Do the bushes look very worn and perished? A test drive will show if this is the case – a poor ride, knocks, squeaks, and creaks! A certain amount of surface rust may be present and is acceptable, or you may be lucky, and have a car whose components have been rust proofed. Bent wishbones are a sure sign of accident damage.

Front & rear subframe

Check the front and rear subframes for heavy corrosion.

Anti-roll bars

Check that the front and rear anti-roll bars are straight, with no damage. Look for worn or perished bushes. Non-standard anti-roll bars may be a different colour than the standard black; if they are, they may also have extra adjustment holes. Check the droplinks, again checking the bushes, ensuring everything is attached together. You may notice surface rust, and this will often be the case on an older car, but be wary of components that appear heavily corroded.

Inner rear wheelarch

Here you'll find one of the key MoT checks for corrosion failures: the seatbelt anchorage points. Look closely for rust, corrosion, or holes beginning to break through. To get a proper look, you may have to remove the arch lining. Check for

It may be difficult to check into the inner rear wheelarches, as a liner will be in place, but this is a key area for corrosion on MX-5s. Check the MoT history for any advisories in this area.

previous repairs, and ascertain their quality. This is one area where the road dirt will really stick, so be prepared to get a little dirty to get a good look.

Exhaust ④ ③ ② ①

MX5s sit low to the ground, and the exhaust can often take quite a bit of punishment in the form of dents and scrapes. Take a look underneath, if you can, to gauge the quality of the exhaust. Is there any damage? If there are any noticeable areas of corrosion or leaks, it may be worth considering a new system. There's plenty of choice, and prices start at about ●x200 for a cat-back stainless steel exhaust – but factor this into the price of any offer you decide to make for the car. Sometimes, the catalytic converter is swapped out for a de-cat pipe, but keep in mind that this may effect emissions and your MoT. If the car you're looking at is a pre-1994 import, then the emissions tolerances are slightly higher, and allow for de-cat pipes. A post-1994 car may experience difficulties with

A full stainless steel exhaust system fitted to a MkI car.

A stainless steel aftermarket exhaust manifold. This is on a 1.8.

a de-cat pipe, and a catalytic converter may need to be sourced (the best option for this is a secondhand cat – brand new ones can be pricey).

The heat shields underneath are known for working loose, and rattling when the car is running. If you're looking at a BBR Turbo model, be sure to check the manifold, and ensure that there are no cracks. These are caused by the manifold not being able to expand evenly with the intensity of the heating and cooling (you may need to take off the heat shield to check this properly).

Catalytic converters are often replaced with de-cat pipes on the early MkI cars.

Engine start up

Start the engine. Does it start first time? If not, there could be any number of reasons for this; if you're not mechanically minded, you may wish to walk away. The MX-5 has hydraulic lash adjustors (tappits, or HLAs); if you can still hear them after returning from the test drive, the car is more than likely due an oil change. A car that has been standing for a while will often have noisy HLAs, and the symptoms may not clear until proper oil changes have been made and the car is back in regular use. If, despite this, the HLAs remain noisy, it's often because they are old, dirty, and sticky. New ones can be fitted to resolve the issue, should oil changes and regular use not be successful.

One the engine has warmed and been turned off, does the car start well/quickly again after standing?

Car stationary, in neutral & engine running

Once the engine has warmed up, rev the engine slowly, listening for knocking sounds: these could be a sign of worn main bearings or small end bearings (see Test drive). Check that the car idles smoothly. If the idle hunts or suddenly drops to stalling point, it could be that the idle needs to be reset (MX-5s are well known for their idle droop). Squealing belts are often a sign that they're too loose, and may need adjustment.

The idle screw on a MkI 1.8 car. On a 1.6 the screw faces left.

Exhaust smoke

White smoke may indicate water in the cylinders, and is often a sign that the head gasket could be leaking. Blue smoke is an indicator that the valve stem seals are worn (not too difficult a fix for the mechanically minded), or the piston rings require replacing.

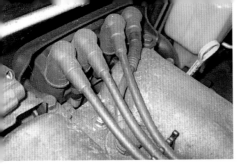

Poor running could be attributed to a faulty coil pack, or the HT leads may need replacing.

Bad tuning on a forced induction car can kill an engine! Detonation has blown away the edges of this piston.

Test drive
Performance

On taking a car for a test drive, try to drive it with the roof up, if possible: you will be able to hear any untoward noises much more clearly.

Be aware of any loss of power, hesitation, or misfire – these are common symptoms indicating that the engine requires either new leads, spark plugs, coil pack, or the timing to be checked and adjusted. At worst, these issues could also point to potential crank failure. It may be better to avoid a car which is not running as it should, unless you are prepared to replace any ancillaries, and have the mechanical know how to resolve its issues. This risk could be mitigated if you decide to test the engine with a compression check. Be aware of any pinking or knock, particularly if you are looking at a car with forced induction. Bad tuning can kill an engine.

Compression check
If you're unsure about the general health of the engine, consider a compression test. This measures the compression in the cylinders. You should be looking for 175-190psi for each cylinder (192psi at 3000rpm is the standard based on a new engine). Values nearer the top of this range are best, however, on a used engine pressure above 135psi is acceptable, with no more than a 28psi difference between cylinders. Always follow the manufacturer's guidelines for these tests.

Clutch

Feel the action of the clutch. Does it engage smoothly? Is there any slippage? The clutch should bite midway; if it's near the top of its travel, the clutch could be worn and may soon need replacing.

If the bite is much lower, or if the operation is stiff, this could indicate a worn clutch slave or master cylinder (also confirmed by low clutch fluid). Replacing the slave or master cylinder isn't expensive, and is easy for the amateur mechanic.

Gearbox
MX-5 gearboxes have been engineered to be one of the highlights of the driving experience. Its precise action should move into gear easily. Check all the gears, and try to use each one several times. If the 'box is a little 'sticky,' it could be due to lack of lubrication of the linkages.

You may notice the gear change is notchy, too, or stiff when cold, particularly in first or second gear.

Whining noises from the gears could indicate worn bearings within the transmission.

Auto gearbox

Some MX-5s were supplied with a four-speed auto 'box. Not hugely popular, as being a pure driver's car, the manual gear change is one of the contributing factors of the MX-5 success story. The auto 'box has no known reliability issues, though you should check the cleanliness of the oil on the dipstick. Smell the oil when the transmission is hot: if it smells at all burnt, walk away and find another. Be aware of any sparkling metallic particles in the oil.

This V-Spec Roadster limited edition is fitted with an auto gearbox.

Differential
Listen for any whining noises. If the differential is nearing the end of its life, you may notice some slack in the drivetrain .

Steering feel
How does the car travel at speed? Are there any noticeable vibrations through the steering wheel, or does the car pull to the left or right? It could be that the wheels need balancing, or that the tracking is out. If the car really doesn't feel right, it could require a geometry reset. This can transform a car and ensures that the car is properly set up for the road.

Suspension feel
Be aware of how the car feels going into corners; does the car wallow, can you hear any noises from the suspension? Worn bushes and leaky shocks can make creaking noises, especially when going over bumps, and can certainly affect the preciseness of the handling.

Brakes
How does the car pull up on braking? Can you feel any vibration through the steering wheel, and does the car stop as it should, and in a straight line? Is there any sponginess in the brake pedal? Any of these symptoms may indicate that the brakes need attention.

Handbrake
Does the handbrake hold the car on an incline? If not, it may need adjustment, or further attention.

Wheels
Listen for any whooshing/whirring noises during the test drive, this may indicate worn wheel bearings

Instrumentation
Ensure everything electrical in the cabin is working: sidelights, main and high beam;

that the headlights on a MkI pop up and go down with no problems; indicators, windscreen wipers, screen washers, and horn. Check that the heater blows hot and cold, and, if the car is fitted with air-con, check that this comes on (with the car running, you'll hear the revs increase as the compressor switches on). However, it may be the case that you don't get any cold air: on early MkIs, R34 refrigerant was used, but this is now illegal and conversions to later refrigerants are costly, so most people don't bother to recharge.

It may not be possible to check the fuel gauge's accuracy until after you've purchased a car. MX-5s don't have a low fuel warning light: if you have a gauge that isn't reading correctly, it's often the fuel sender at fault – an easy, low cost issue to fix.

Speedo & rev counter
Eunos imports may still have the speedo calibrated in km/h, so they'll need to be converted if not done so already. Check during the test drive that it's working

correctly. Any needle bounce may be due to a weak magnet, or the speedo cable may need lubrication.

Oil pressure gauge
Early MkI cars (up until 1994) have a working oil pressure gauge, which reads in psi on UK cars and metric on the Eunos Roadsters, and gives the true engine oil pressure. When the car is revved, you'll see the needle move. Cars from '94 onward came with a faux gauge, which only shows that there is some pressure, and will remain in a fixed position until the engine is turned off. For the cars with the early gauges, with the engine running, the oil pressure should read high when the engine is cold. Once warm, check it drops to 2.5-3.0 kg/cm (which is around the 30-60lb/in mark on UK models). On the faux gauge, it should read just over halfway.

Oil pressure gauge on a Eunos Roadster

Oil pressure gauge as seen on 1994 cars onwards. These are 'dummy' gauges.

Water temperature gauge

The temperature gauge should warm to just left of centre: keep checking this on the test drive to ensure this remains the same throughout. If it goes much higher, there's a cooling issue.

Immobiliser/alarm

A must for a convertible car, and, more often than not, insurance premiums for MX-5s without a security device are costly, so it's a worthwhile investment. Generally, you'll find most will have an immobiliser, alarm, or both already fitted, so check the system is working. It's also handy to check if the fitting certificate is included with the car's history; you'll need to know the make and model for insurance purposes, or should a spare alarm/immobiliser fob be required.

Temperature gauge on a MkI, reading at its ideal level.

Number/licence plates

Check they are secure, and that the number plate is legible and legal.

Vehicle identification numbers

The VINs can be found on a plate in the engine bay, on the firewall (bulkhead). They can also be found on the driver's side door shut, on a white sticker (although this is sometimes removed, especially if a car has been resprayed). The VIN for UK cars start JMZ. For Japanese Eunos Roadsters, they start NA.

MkI and MkII engine numbers are difficult to spot, but reside on the rear of the block, on the passenger side nearest the firewall, the VIN is also stamped to the oil pan on 1.6 and 1.8 models. Be sure to double check the VINs against the V5 documentation.

Paperwork

Ensure the V5 log book or ownership documentation, and the relevant roadworthiness certificate, is in place for the car (MoT in UK, TÜV in Germany, Contrôle Technique in France, and in the USA, each state has its own vehicle test requirements).

A full service history is always beneficial, and it's worth checking it to see what expenses have been lavished (or not!) on the car. For UK cars, if you can, check any previous MoT failures and/or advisories to gauge what work has been carried out on the car, and what may still need to be done.

Evaluation procedure

Add up the total points score: 296 = perfect; 222 = good; 148 = average; 74 = poor. Cars scoring over 207 should be completely usable and require the minimum of repair or rectification, although continued service maintenance and care will be required to keep them in good condition. Cars scoring between 74 and 151 will require serious work (at much the same cost regardless of score). Cars scoring between 152 and 206 will require very careful assessment of the necessary repair costs in order to reach a realistic resale value.

10 Auctions
– sold! Another way to buy your dream

Auction pros & cons

Pros: Prices are usually lower than those of dealers or private sellers and you might grab a real bargain on the day. Auctioneers have usually established clear title with the seller. At the venue you can usually examine documentation relating to the vehicle.

Cons: You have to rely on a sketchy catalogue description of condition and history. The opportunity to inspect is limited and you cannot drive the car. Auction cars are often a little below par and may require some work. It's easy to overbid. There will usually be a buyer's premium to pay in addition to the auction hammer price.

Which auction?

Auctions by established auctioneers are advertised in car magazines and on the auction houses' websites. A catalogue, or a simple printed list of the lots for auctions might only be available a day or two ahead, though often lots are listed and pictured on auctioneers' websites much earlier. Contact the auction company to ask if previous auction selling prices are available as this is useful information (details of past sales are often available on websites).

Catalogue, entry fee and payment details

When you purchase the catalogue of the vehicles in the auction, it often acts as a ticket allowing two people to attend the viewing days and the auction. Catalogue details tend to be comparatively brief, but will include information such as 'one owner from new, low mileage, full service history,' etc. It will also usually show a guide price to give you some idea of what to expect to pay and will tell you what is charged as a 'Buyer's premium.' The catalogue will also contain details of acceptable forms of payment. At the fall of the hammer an immediate deposit is usually required, the balance payable within 24 hours. If the plan is to pay by cash there may be a cash limit. Some auctions will accept payment by debit card. Sometimes credit or charge cards are acceptable, but will often incur an extra charge. A bank draft or bank transfer will have to be arranged in advance with your own bank as well as with the auction house. No car will be released before all payments are cleared. If delays occur in payment transfers then storage costs can accrue.

Buyer's premium

A buyer's premium will be added to the hammer price: don't forget this in your calculations. It is not usual for there to be a further state tax or local tax on the purchase price and/or on the buyer's premium.

Viewing

In some instances it's possible to view on the day, or days before, as well as in the hours prior to, the auction. There are auction officials available who are willing to help out by opening engine and luggage compartments and to allow you to inspect the interior. While the officials may start the engine for you, a test drive is out of the question. Crawling under and around the car as much as you want is permitted, but you can't suggest that the car you are interested in be jacked up, or attempt to do the job yourself. You can also ask to see any documentation available.

Bidding

Before you take part in the auction, decide your maximum bid – and stick to it!

It may take a while for the auctioneer to reach the lot you are interested in, so use that time to observe how other bidders behave. When it's the turn of your car, attract the auctioneer's attention and make an early bid. The auctioneer will then look to you for a reaction every time another bid is made, usually the bids will be in fixed increments until the bidding slows, when smaller increments will often be accepted before the hammer falls. If you want to withdraw from the bidding, make sure the auctioneer understands your intentions – a vigorous shake of the head when he or she looks to you for the next bid should do the trick!

Assuming that you are the successful bidder, the auctioneer will note your card or paddle number, and from that moment on you will be responsible for the vehicle.

If the car is unsold, either because it failed to reach the reserve or because there was little interest, it may be possible to negotiate with the owner, via the auctioneers, after the sale is over.

Successful bid

There are two more items to think about. How to get the car home, and insurance. If you can't drive the car, your own or a hired trailer is one way, another is to have the vehicle shipped using the facilities of a local company. The auction house will also have details of companies specialising in the transfer of cars.

Insurance for immediate cover can usually be purchased on site, but it may be more cost-effective to make arrangements with your own insurance company in advance, and then call to confirm the full details.

eBay & other online auctions

eBay and other online auctions could land you a car at a bargain price, though you'd be foolhardy to bid without examining the car first, something most vendors encourage. A useful feature of eBay is that the geographical location of the car is shown, so you can narrow your choices to those within a realistic radius of home. Be prepared to be outbid in the last few moments of the auction. Remember, your bid is binding and that it will be very, very difficult to get restitution in the case of a crooked vendor fleecing you – caveat emptor!

Be aware that some cars offered for sale in online auctions are 'ghost' cars. Don't part with any cash without being sure that the vehicle does actually exist and is as described (usually pre-bidding inspection is possible).

Auctioneers

Barrett-Jackson:
www.barrett-jackson.com.
Bonhams: www.bonhams.com
British Car Auctions (BCA):
www.bca-europe.com or
www.british-car-auctions.co.uk
Cheffins: www.cheffins.co.uk

Christies: www.christies.com
Coys: www.coys.co.uk
eBay: www.eBay.com
H&H: www.classic-auctions.co.uk
RM: www.rmauctions.com
Shannons: www.shannons.com.au
Silver: www.silverauctions.com

11 Paperwork
– correct documentation is essential!

Classic, collector and prestige cars usually come with a large portfolio of paperwork accumulated and passed on by a succession of proud owners. This documentation represents the real history of the car and from it can be deduced the level of care the car has received, how much it's been used, which specialists have worked on it and the dates of major repairs and restorations. All of this information will be priceless to you as the new owner, so be very wary of cars with little paperwork to support their claimed history.

Registration documents
All countries/states have some form of registration for private vehicles whether it's like the American 'pink slip' system or the British 'log book' system.

It is essential to check that the registration document is genuine, that it relates to the car in question, and that all the vehicle's details are correctly recorded, including chassis/VIN and engine numbers (if these are shown). If you are buying from the previous owner, his or her name and address will be recorded in the document: this will not be the case if you are buying from a dealer.

In the UK the current (Euro-aligned) registration document is named V5C, and is printed in coloured sections of blue, green and pink. The blue section relates to the car specification, the green section has details of the new owner and the pink section is sent to the DVLA in the UK when the car is sold. A small section in yellow deals with selling the car within the motor trade.

In the UK the DVLA will provide details of earlier keepers of the vehicle upon payment of a small fee, and much can be learned in this way.

If the car has a foreign registration there may be expensive and time-consuming formalities to complete. Do you really want the hassle?

Roadworthiness certificate
Most country/state administrations require that vehicles are regularly tested to prove that they are safe to use on the public highway and do not produce excessive emissions. In the UK that test (the 'MoT') is carried out at approved testing stations, for a fee. In the USA the requirement varies, but most states insist on an emissions test every two years as a minimum, while the police are charged with pulling over unsafe-looking vehicles.

In the UK the test is required on an annual basis once a vehicle becomes three years old. Of particular relevance for older cars is that the certificate issued includes the mileage reading recorded at the test date and, therefore, becomes an independent record of that car's history. Ask the seller if previous certificates are available. Without an MoT the vehicle should be trailored to its new home, unless you insist that a valid MoT is part of the deal. (Not such a bad idea this, as at least you will know the car was roadworthy on the day it was tested and you don't need to wait for the old certificate to expire before having the test done.)

Road licence
The administration of every country/state charges some kind of tax for the use of its road system, the actual form of the 'road licence,' and how it is displayed, varying enormously country to country and state to state.

Whatever the form of the 'road licence,' it must relate to the vehicle carrying it and must be present and valid if the car is to be driven on the public highway legally. The value of the license will depend on the length of time it will continue to be valid.

In the UK if a car is untaxed because it has not been used for a period of time, the owner has to inform the licensing authorities, otherwise the vehicle's date-related registration number will be lost and there will be a painful amount of paperwork to get it re-registered.

Certificates of authenticity

For many makes of collectible car it is possible to get a certificate proving the age and authenticity (eg engine and VIN/chassis numbers, paint colour and trim) of a particular vehicle, these are called 'Heritage Certificates' and in the case of the XK can be acquired from the Jaguar Heritage Trust in Coventry, UK. If the car comes with one of these it is a definite bonus. If you want to obtain one, contact the Trust via www.jdht.com

Valuation certificate

Hopefully, the vendor will have a recent valuation certificate, or letter signed by a recognised expert stating how much he, or she, believes the particular car to be worth (such documents, together with photos, are usually needed to get 'agreed value' insurance). Generally such documents should act only as confirmation of your own assessment of the car rather than a guarantee of value as the expert has probably not seen the car in the flesh. The easiest way to find out how to obtain a formal valuation is to contact the owners' club.

Service history

Often, older cars will have been serviced at home by enthusiastic (and hopefully capable) owners for a good number of years. Nevertheless, try to obtain as much service history and other paperwork pertaining to the car as you can. Naturally, dealer stamps, or specialist garage receipts score most points in the value stakes. However, anything helps in the great authenticity game, items like the original bill of sale, handbook, parts invoices and repair bills, adding to the story and the character of the car. Even a brochure correct to the year of the car's manufacture is a useful document, and something that you could well have to search hard to locate in future years. If the seller claims that the car has been restored, then expect receipts and other evidence from a specialist restorer.

If the seller claims to have carried out regular servicing, ask what work was completed, when, and seek some evidence of it being carried out. Your assessment of the car's overall condition should tell you whether the seller's claims are genuine.

Restoration photographs

If the seller tells you that the car has been restored (or, more appropriately in the case of these quite modern cars, refurbished), then expect to be shown a series of photographs taken while the work was under way. Pictures taken at various stages, and from various angles, should help you gauge the thoroughness of the work. If you buy the car, ask if you can have all the photographs, as they form an important part of the vehicle's history. It's surprising how many sellers are happy to part with their car and accept your cash, but want to hang on to their photographs! In the latter event, you may be able to persuade the vendor to get a set of copies made.

12 What's it worth?
– let your head rule your heart

Condition

If the car you've been looking at is really bad, then you've probably not bothered to use the marking system in chapter 9 – '60 minute evaluation.' You may not have even got as far as using that chapter at all!

If you did use the marking system in chapter 9, you'll know whether the car is in Excellent (maybe Concours), Good, Average or Poor condition or, perhaps, somewhere in-between these categories.

Many car magazines run a regular price guide. If you haven't bought the latest issues, do so now and compare their suggested values for the model you are thinking of buying: also look at the auction prices they're reporting. Some models will always be more sought-after than others. Trends can change, too. The published values tend to vary from one magazine to another, as do the scales of condition, so read the guidance notes carefully. Bear in mind that a car that is in truly magnificent condition or even a recent show winner, could be worth more than the highest scale published. Assuming the car you have in mind is not in show/Concours condition, then relate the level of condition that you judge the car to be in with the appropriate guide price. How does the figure compare with the asking price? Before you start haggling with the seller, consider what affect any variation from standard specification might have on the car's value.

If you are buying from a dealer, remember there will be a dealer's premium on the price.

Desirable options/extras

Special/limited edition cars – particularly for their performance modifications, such as suspension, alloy wheels, uprated anti-roll bars, lightened flywheel, and interior cabin finishes.
Torsen limited-slip differential
Hardtop
Mohair hood
Leather interior
Metallic paint
Electric windows
Electric mirrors
Air-conditioning

Below is a list of some of the limited and special editions, in order of their appearance, detailing year, paintwork colour and, if applicable, number of models produced. Limited editions have a predefined production volume (shown in brackets), and special editions are production models with non-standard features. This is not an exhaustive list, but contains those models most likely to be encountered for sale.

UK
Mkl 1.6
1990/91 BBR Turbo: various colours (not believed to be over 200)
1991 24 Hour Le Mans: 24 Hour Le Mans Green/Orange/White Paintwork (24)

1991 Limited Edition (LE): Neo Green (250)
1992/93 Special Equipment (SE) Version 1: Brilliant Black (200)
1993/94 Special Equipment (SE) Version 2: Brilliant Black (150)
1995 California: Sunburst Yellow (300)
1996/97 Monaco: Neo Green (450)
1997 Monza: Neo Green (800)

Mkl 1.8
1995/96 Gleneagles: Montego Blue (400)
1996 Merlot: Vin Rouge Merlot (600)
1997 Dakar: Twilight Blue (400)
1997 Harvard: Silver Stone (500)
1997 Classic: Brilliant Black (400)
1998 Berkeley: Sparkle Green (400)

MkII 1.6
2000 California: Sunburst Yellow (500)
2000 Isola: Classic Red (500)

MKII 1.8
1998/99 Sport: Classic Red (300)
1999 Sport: Racing Blue (300)
1999 10th Anniversary: Innocent Blue (600 UK, 3700 Europe)
2000 Jasper Conran: Platinum (100), Classic Black (400)
2000 Icon: Vin Rouge Merlot (750)

USA
Mkl 1.6
1991 Special Edition: Racing Green (4000)
1992 Sunburst Yellow: colour as name (1500)

Mkl 1.8
1994 Limited Edition: Brilliant Black (1500)
1994 M Edition: Montego Blue (3000)
1994/95 Laguna Blue: Colour As Name (463)
1995 M Edition: Vin Rouge Merlot (3500)
1996 M Edition: Starlight (2968)
1997 M Edition: Excellent Green (3000)
1997 STO: Twilight Blue (1500)

MkII 1.8
1999 10th Anniversary: Innocent Blue (3150)
2001 Special Edition: British Racing Green (3000)

Japan
Mkl 1.6
1990 92 V-Special: Neo Green/Brilliant Black
1991 J-Limited: Sunburst Yellow (800)
    M2-1001: Brave Blue (300)

M2-1002: Brave Blue (300)
1992 93 S-Special: Brilliant Black/Classic Red/Chaste White
1992 S-Limited: Brilliant Black (1000)
1993 Tokyo Limited: Brilliant Black (40)

MkI 1.8
1993 V-Special II: Neo Green/Brilliant Black
1993 J-Limited II: Sunburst Yellow (800)
1994-96 S-Special II: Brilliant Black/Classic Red/Laguna Blue/Chaste White/
Montego Blue
1994 M2-1028: Brilliant Black/Chaste White (300)
1994 RS-Limited: Montego Blue (500)
1995 G-Limited: Satellite Blue (1500)
1995 R-Limited: Satellite Blue (894), Chaste White (106)
1995/96 VR-Limited Combination A: Vin Rouge Merlot (700)
1995 VR-Limited Comination B: Excellent Green (800)
1996 B2-Limited: Twilight Blue (1000)
1996 R2-Limited: Chaste White (500)
1997 SR-Limited: Sparkle Green (700)

MkII 1.8
1998 RS: Evolution Orange, Brilliant Black, Twilight Blue, Racing Silver, Highlight/
Racing Silver, Classic Red, Chaste White
1999 10th Anniversary: Innocent Blue (1000)
2000 NR-Limited: Vin Rouge Merlot (500)
2000 YS-Limited: Brilliant Black, Pure White, Sunlight Silver (700)

Undesirable features
Non-original paintwork
Detuned 1.6 engine
Automatic gearbox
Over-the-top bodykits
Oversize alloy wheels (17in plus)

Striking a deal
Negotiate on the basis of your condition assessment, mileage, and fault rectification
cost. Also take into account the car's specification. Be realistic about the value, but
don't be completely intractable: a small compromise on the part of the vendor or
buyer will often facilitate a deal at little real cost.

13 Do you really want to restore?
– it'll take longer and cost more than you think

The bare MkI MX-5 chassis. Here you can see the powerplant frame connecting the gearbox with the differential.

At the time this book was published, the oldest MX-5s were 22 years old. They're certainly not difficult to restore, as there's a plethora of new and secondhand parts available, and as they're often used as a base for kit cars, pretty much everything can be disassembled, and it's not too complicated to rebuild. For most people looking to restore, the issue to consider is the time it may take to complete: what initially may appear to be a minor restoration, could be more than anticipated, particularly if the rust has taken hold, and structural problems have been uncovered. Other factors are whether you have the space to store and work on the car, the technical tools, and – most importantly – the know-how, mechanical knowledge, and expertise.

Most MX-5s aren't (yet!) so far gone that they require a full nut and bolt restoration, although I have known of cars so rotten with rust that owners have reshelled them. This is probably the most difficult and time-consuming job of them all, as so much needs to be swapped over. If the rust is only affecting the sills or rear arches, parts suppliers now sell brand new steel repair sections, for the inner and outer sill and rear arch areas.

Another common and popular restoration project, is to overhaul the under-chassis of the car. This entails cleaning and wirebrushing the underneath of the car, treating any rust, undersealing, and rustproofing all exposed areas. Even the wishbones, anti-roll bars and drop links must be removed for rustproofing, and re-bushing with either polybushes or new rubber

What looks like just a few paint bubbles ...

... once cut back shows just how established the rust is on the rear sills of this MkI.

The rear sills on this MkI need some serious attention, and although this does look incredibly severe, it is repairable. Cars in worse condition than this have been successfully restored, but it does take hard work and the right craftsmanship to make good.

bushes (the consensus is that polybushes give a far harsher ride), and finally wax-oyling all cavities.

For vehicles looking tired and worn on the interior, carpet sets are available new or secondhand. Specialist trimmers, who have much experience working on MX-5s, can also replace the original vinyl soft top (with the same or in mohair), and retrim the interior. Cabin plastics can often fade, crack, and break over time, but there are options to replace with either secondhand or brand new pieces.

Restoration is all about the budget: this decides how far you can go with your project. There's even the option to replace like-for-like with all brand new, if you so wish.

If you're considering a restoration of any kind – whether chassis, bodywork, engine, or otherwise – there are many owners who have done it all before: seek the advice of club and forum members who have such experience and knowledge.

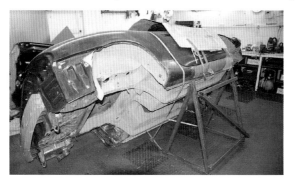

This is a MkII totally stripped back, and the subject of a complete refresh, which included rust treatment, welding, rustproofing. This kind of project is not for the faint hearted!

To ensure the longevity of the suspension components, owners will often treat and rustproof the wishbones, and rebush with either polythene or rubber bushes.

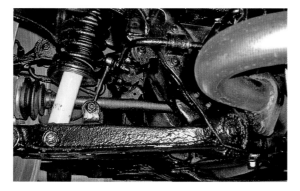

A MkII car that has been completely rustproofed and undersealed throughout on the chassis. This should certainly keep any corrosion at bay, but if you are planning on keeping the car for any length of time, it's wise to maintain the rustproofing process; schedule one in every few years.

– bad complexion, including dimples, pimples and bubbles

Paint faults generally occur due to lack of protection and/or maintenance, or to poor preparation prior to a respray or touch-up. Some of the following conditions may be present in the car you're looking at.

Orange peel
This appears as an uneven paint surface, similar to the appearance of the skin of an orange. The fault is caused by the failure of atomized paint droplets to flow into each other when they hit a surface. It's sometimes possible to rub out the effect with proprietary paint cutting/rubbing compound or very fine grades of abrasive paper. A respray may be necessary in severe

Orange peel.

cases. Consult a bodywork repairer/paint shop for advice on the particular car.

If the paint is cracking ...

... or crazing, paint removal and respraying will be required.

Cracking
Severe cases are likely to have been caused by too heavy an application of paint (or filler beneath the paint). Also, insufficient stirring of the paint before application can lead to the components being improperly mixed, and cracking can result. Incompatibility with the paint already on the panel can have a similar effect. To rectify the problem it's necessary to rub down to a smooth, sound finish before respraying the problem area.

Crazing
Sometimes the paint takes on a crazed rather than a cracked appearance when the problems mentioned under 'Cracking' are present. This problem can also be caused by a reaction between the underlying surface and the paint. Paint removal and respraying the problem area is usually the only solution.

Blistering
Almost always caused by corrosion of the metal beneath the paint. Usually perforation will be found in the metal and the damage will usually be worse than that suggested by the area of blistering. The metal will have to be repaired before repainting.

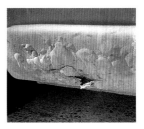

It's not difficult to see that rust has caused blistering here.

Micro blistering

Usually the result of an economy respray where inadequate heating has allowed moisture to settle on the car before spraying. Consult a paint specialist, but usually damaged paint will have to be removed before partial or full respraying. Can also be caused by car covers that don't 'breathe.'

Micro blistering ...

Red paint can be particularly prone to fading.

Fading

Some colours, especially reds, are prone to fading if subjected to strong sunlight for long periods without the benefit of polish protection. Sometimes proprietary paint restorers and/or paint cutting/rubbing compounds will retrieve the situation. Often a respray is the only real solution.

Peeling

Often a problem with metallic paintwork when the sealing lacquer becomes damaged and begins to peel off. Poorly applied paint may also peel. The remedy is to strip and start again!

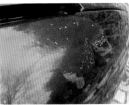

... and peeling ...

Dimples

Dimples in the paintwork are caused by the residue of polish (particularly silicone types) not being removed properly before respraying. Paint removal and repainting is the only solution.

Dents

Small dents are usually easily cured by the 'Dentmaster,' or equivalent process, that sucks or pushes out the dent (as long as the paint surface is still intact). Companies offering dent removal services usually come to your home: consult your telephone directory.

... often occur together.

15 Problems due to lack of use
– just like their owners, MX-5s need exercise!

When considering an MX-5 that may have been stood for a while, these problems may be present.

Seized components
Callipers, slave and master cylinders can seize.

The clutch may seize if the plate becomes stuck to the flywheel because of corrosion.

Handbrakes can seize if the cables and linkages rust.

Pistons can seize in the bores due to corrosion. Bonnet hinges can rust up and seize.

An MX-5 that has been standing for a while will often have noisy HLAs/tappets, the symptoms of which may not clear until proper oil changes have been made, and the car is back in regular use.

Seized callipers can be taken apart and reconditioned, or alternatively new units can be purchased. This is the one component most likely to be affected should an MX-5 be left to stand for a considerable amount of time.

Fluids
Old, acidic oil can corrode bearings.

Uninhibited coolant can corrode internal waterways. Lack of antifreeze can cause core plugs to be pushed out, or even cracks in the block or head. Silt settling and solidifying can cause overheating.

Brake fluid absorbs water from the atmosphere and should be renewed every two years. Old fluid with a high water content can cause corrosion and pistons/ calipers to seize (freeze), and can also also cause brake failure when the water turns to vapour near hot braking components,

It's inevitable that the tyres will lose their pressure on a car that's been stood up. It's best not to let them get to this state, as the tyre wall and wheel rim are easily damaged.

Tyre problems
Tyres that have had the weight of the car on them in a single position for some time will develop flat spots, resulting in some (usually temporary) vibration. The tyre walls may have cracks or (blister-type) bulges, meaning new tyres are needed.

Shock absorbers (dampers)
With lack of use, the dampers will lose their elasticity, or even seize. Creaking, groaning and stiff suspension are signs of this problem.

Bodywork
Paintwork will fade, dull, and lose its

lustre if kept outside or anywhere damp. Rust will start to take hold, especially so if the drainholes in the sills become blocked, leaving water to pool.

The soft top will deteriorate and weather, and the hood drain holes are likely to become blocked, and possibly flood water back into the cabin, causing damp and mould on the seats, carpets and inside of the roof.

This is the state of the rear sills on a MkI Roadster that had been stood for about two years. The rust has completely holed the outer sill.

Rubber and plastic
Radiator hoses may have perished and split, possibly resulting in the loss of all coolant. Window and door seals can harden and leak. Gaitors/boots can crack. Wiper blades will harden.

Electrics
MX-5 batteries can drain very quickly, and they are likely to be of little use if they haven't been charged for many months.

Earthing/grounding problems are common when connections have corroded.

Sparkplug electrodes will often have corroded in an unused engine.

Wiring insulation can harden and fail.

Moisure will eventually get into the cabin on an MX-5. Sometimes it can only take a couple of weeks for the mould and mildew to take over, from just the slightest amount of condensation. The roof (as is the case here), seats, carpet and other interior components can become covered, and will require treating with a fungicide to get rid of the spores and prevent them returning.

Exhaust
Exhaust gas contains a high water content, so exhaust systems corrode very quickly from the inside when the car is not used, particularly if made from mild steel.

16 The Community
– key people, organisations and companies in the MX-5 world

Clubs & forums
Club Roadster
www.clubroadster.com

Mazda MX-5 Community
www.MX-5.com

Miata.net
www.miata.net

MX5Nutz
www.mx5nutz.com

MX-5 Owners' club UK
www.mx5oc.co.uk

UK repairers, specialists (incluing breakers) and dealers
AK Automotive. Newcastle. Tel: 01207 544071
Autolink. Southampton, Hants. Tel: 01489 877770 www.autolinkuk.co.uk
CBS Autos. Nelson, Lancs Tel: 01282 697413 www.mx5specialists.com
Dandy Cars. Ilford, Essex Tel: 0845 450 4589 www.dandycars.com
Deepcar Autobodies Ltd, Unit 50, Wharncliffe Ind Est, Station Road, Sheffield
S36 2UZ Tel: 0114 2838900/07800655903
Goodwood Sports Cars. Berwick Upon Tweed, Tel: 01289 305735
www.goodwoodsportscars.co.uk
Mazda UK. Tel: 08458 505605 www.mazda.co.uk
MX5 Heaven. Dorchester, Dorset, Tel: 01305 268149 www.mx5heaven.co.uk
MX5 City. Doncaster, Tel: 0845 2300 957 www.mx5city.com
Performance 5. Middlesex Tel: 0845 230 4505 www.performance5.com
Sam Goodwin. Nuneaton, Warwickshire Tel: 024 7635 3909
www.samgoodwin.com
5 Speed. Hucknall, Nottingham Tel: 01159 642102 www.5-speed.co.uk

UK parts and accessory suppliers
Moss Europe. Tel: 0208 867 2020 www.mossmx5.co.uk
MX-5 Parts. Tel: 0845 325 2384 www.mx5parts.co.uk
SFT MX5 Parts. Tel: 0121 544 5555 www.davidmanners.co.uk
TR Lane Fabrications. Tel: 07790 723639 www.trlane.co.uk

US spares, specialists and parts websites
Autokonexion. www.autokonexion.com
Duetto Motors. www.duettomotors.com
Flyin Miata. www.flyinmiata.com
Hard Dog Fabrication. www.bethania-garage.com
Miata Roadster. www.miataroadster.com

MM Miata. www.mmmiata.com
R Speed. www.rspeed.net
Rev9 Autosport. www.rev9autosport.com
Track Dog Racing. www.trackdogracing.com

International spares, specialist and parts websites
IL Motorsport. Germany www.ilmotorsport.de
KG Works. Japan www.kgworks.co.jp
Zoom Engineering. Japan www.zoom-eng.com

Soft top fitters, suppliers and trimmers
Jack Smiths Trimmers. Swansea, Tel: 01792 461022
Hot Hoods. Romford, Essex Tel: 07957 273270 www.hothoods.co.uk
Mazmania. Knutsford Tel: 07812 152250 www.mazmania.co.uk
Prestige Car Hoods. Tel: 0151 643 9555 www.prestigecarhoods.com

Geometry setting/wheel alignment specialists
Wheels In Motion. Tel 01494 797825 www.wheels-inmotion.co.uk

Motorsports
www.good-win-racing.com
www.ma5daracing.com
www.max5racing.com
www.mazdaontrack.co.uk

Books
Mazda MX-5 Miata 1.6 Enthusiasts Workshop Manual by Rod Grainger.
ISBN 9781845840839. Veloce Publishing.
Mazda MX-5 Miata 1.8 Enthusiasts Workshop Manual by Rod Grainger.
ISBN 9781845840907. Veloce Publishing.

17 Vital statistics
– essential data at your fingertips

Common specifications
Engine: Inline four-cylinder water cooled double overhead cam 16-valve longitudinal
Suspension: Double wishbone front and rear, coil springs
Transmission: Five-speed manual, rear-wheel drive
Steering: Rack and pinion
Wheels: 4x100pcd, 5.5jx14 185/60/14 or 6jx15 195/50/15

MkI 1.6 1989–1995
Displacement: 1598cc. Max power, revs/torque: 116bhp @ 6500rpm/100lb/ft @
5500rpm. 0-60mph: 8.7 seconds. Top speed: 121mph. Brakes: 235mm (f) and
231mm (r) discs. Weight: 950kg/2094lb. Fuel tank: 45 litres.

MkI 1.6 1995-1998 UK only
Max power, revs/torque: 90bhp @ 6000rpm/97lb/ft at 4000rpm

MkI 1.8 1993-1995
Displacement: 1839cc. Max power, revs/torque: 130bhp @ 6500rpm/110lb/ft @
5000rpm 0-60mph: 8.5 seconds. Top speed: 120mph. Brakes: 254mm (f) and
251mm (r) discs. Weight: 1020kg/2248lb.

Additional revisions to 1.8 from mid 1996
Max power, revs/torque: 131bhp @ 6500rpm/114lb/ft @ 5000rpm. 0-60mph: 8.6
seconds. Top speed: 123mph.

MkII 1.6 1998-2001
Displacement: 1597cc. Max power, revs/torque: 110bhp @ 6500rpm/99lb/ft @
5500rpm. 0-60mph: 9.7 seconds. Top speed: 118mph. Brakes: 255mm (f) and
251mm (r) discs. Weight: 1025kg/2259lb. Fuel tank: 45 litres.

MkII 1.8 1998-2001
As 1.6 with following revisions:
Displacement: 1839cc. Max power, revs/torque: 140bhp @ 6500rpm/119lb/ft @
5500rpm. 0-60mph: 7.8 seconds. Top speed: 127mph. Transmission: five-speed
manual (six speed on 10th AE, RS and VS editions).

MX-5 standard colours
MkI: Classic Red, Brilliant Black, Crystal White, Mariner Blue, Silver Stone Metallic
MkII: Classic Red, Green Metallic, Bronze, Silver Metallic, Black

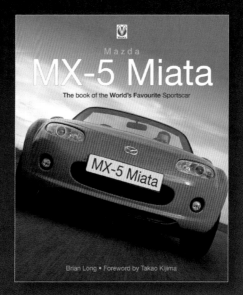

Mazda MX-5 Miata 1.6
Enthusiast's Workshop Manual
Rod Grainger & Pete Shoemark

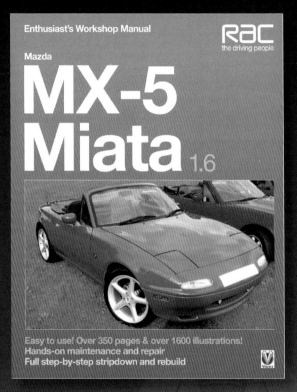

ISBN 978-1-845840-83-9
Paperback • 27x21cm • £25.00* UK / $49.95* US
368 pages • 1600+ pictures

Friendly and easy to understand. Covers all 1989-1994 1.6 models,
including Eunos. Rod stripped down an MX-5 in a domestic garage using
ordinary tools and took over 1500 step-by-step photos. Details every
aspect of all the important jobs.

*prices subject to change, p&p extra.
For more details visit www.veloce.co.uk or email info@veloce.co.uk

Mazda MX-5 Miata 1.8

Enthusiast's Workshop Manual
Rod Grainger & Pete Shoemark

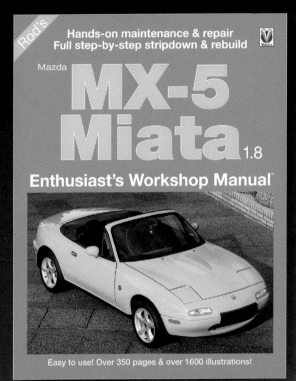

Rod's

Hands-on maintenance & repair
Full step-by-step stripdown & rebuild

Mazda

MX-5
Miata 1.8

Enthusiast's Workshop Manual

Easy to use! Over 350 pages & over 1600 illustrations!

ISBN 978-1-845840-90-7
Paperback • 25x20.7cm • £25.00* UK / $49.95* US
368 pages • 1600+ pictures

Covers all MX-5, Miata & Eunos 1.8 models from 1994 (all cars with pop-up headlights). • Just like its predecessor this new book is phenomenally detailed, informative, helpful and easy to understand. Every detail of important repair and maintenance jobs is covered, including how to overcome problems without resorting to special tools.

*prices subject to change, p&p extra.
For more details visit www.veloce.co.uk or email info@veloce.co.uk

Roads with a View
England's greatest views and how to find them by road
David Corfield

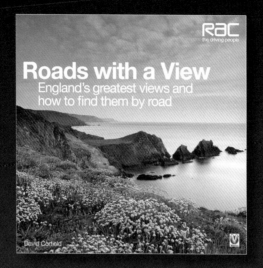

ISBN 978-1-845843-50-2
Hardback • 25x25cm • £19.99* UK / $45* US
• 44 pages • 57 pictures

Roads with a View is not just another travel guide. This one has been
written by a driver especially for fellow motorists, and provides detailed
accounts of the best roads to drive on, and the best places to drive to
for that stunning front seat view. With specially drawn maps, stunningly
beautiful colour photography from some of the England's finest landscape
photographers, and plenty of travel advice on where to eat, where to stay,
and what to do, this unique guide lifts the lid on parts of England that are
often overlooked. The author has made sure to include information for
everyone – driver as well as passengers – as you seek out England's finest
landscapes. With advice on where to stay and where to eat, as well as
what to do when you get to the view, this really is an invaluable travel guide.

*prices subject to change, p&p extra.
For more details visit www.veloce.co.uk or email info@veloce.co.uk

Index